BEYOND THE SPECTRUM

INSPIRING STORIES OF INDIVIDUALS WITH AUTISM

For bulk orders, please visit talesofgreatness.com

Book Design by HMDPublishing.com

THIS BOOK BELONGS TO:

____

PREFACE

For too long, autism has been misunderstood. Too often, the focus is on the challenges that people with autism face, while their talents are overlooked. This book aims to change that by sharing tales of incredible people who prove that autism isn't an obstacle, but a source of strength and achievement.

The people in these pages faced many challenges. They turned those challenges into opportunities and built incredible lives. They pushed beyond what others thought was impossible. They defied expectations. They focused on their strengths and created something remarkable. Some lift the heaviest weights on earth. Some write words that travel across the globe. Some unlock the mysteries of science, solve the toughest math problems, or heal others through medicine. Some see patterns and sounds in ways most of us never will. They are inspiring. They are extraordinary. They are beyond the spectrum.

This book is about what happens when someone is given the chance to do what they do best. The tales in these pages focus on talent and brilliance instead of limitations. They show us what happens when the world stops trying to change people and instead lets them shine.

As you read these tales, I hope they remind you of one simple truth: Greatness doesn't follow the usual path.

CONTENTS

PROTECT OUR FUTURE
PROTECT OUR FUTURE
PROTECT OUR FUTURE
PROTECT OUR FUTURE
PROTECT OUR FUTURE

GRETA THUNBERG
CLIMATE ACTIVIST

Greta Thunberg stood under bright stage lights, looking out at hundreds of faces staring back at her. She took a deep breath and spoke clearly and bravely. "Our planet needs our help right now," she told the crowd. Her voice was calm but strong, filling the room with urgency. Everyone listened closely. They could tell this young girl from Sweden cared deeply about the future of our planet.

Greta was born in Stockholm, Sweden, in 2003. When she was 11 years old, she learned about climate change. She couldn't believe how serious the problem was and how little people were doing to stop it. Greta began to think deeply about how humans were harming the planet. Her thoughts often consumed her, and she felt a strong need to act.

When she was diagnosed with autism, Greta didn't see it as a weakness. Instead, she called it her "superpower." Autism gave her the ability to focus on her mission with incredible determination. Greta stayed committed to her goal: saving Earth.

In 2018, at 15 years old, Greta began skipping school on Fridays to protest outside the Swedish Parliament. She held a simple sign that said, "School Strike for Climate." At first, she stood alone, but her passion caught the attention of people around the world. Soon, millions of students joined her in striking for climate change awareness.

Greta's bravery inspired many people to take action. Her autism helped her see clearly what needed to change, and it gave her the strength to never give up. Greta proves that being different can lead to amazing things. She reminds us that when we speak up and stay true to ourselves, we can make the world better.

NASA

ADHARA PÉREZ

ASTROPHYSICS PRODIGY

Adhara Pérez sat on the rooftop of her home in Mexico City, gazing at the stars. The night sky stretched above her like an endless canvas of possibilities. The stars felt close—close enough to touch. She dreamed of reaching them one day.

At school, life was far from easy. Other children whispered as she walked by, their voices sharp and cutting. They didn't understand her, and she didn't understand them. Diagnosed with autism at age three, Adhara faced many challenges. Teachers assumed she couldn't keep up and doubted her abilities. The classroom wasn't designed for her unique mind.

Adhara's mother noticed something that others overlooked, Adhara was undeniably special. At home, she devoured books and solved math problems far beyond her years. Numbers became her language, a steady presence in a chaotic world. By the time she was five, she had completed elementary school. At nine, she graduated from high school. While most kids her age were playing, Adhara was diving into the world of engineering. Science became her universe. Equations, theories, and the mysteries of space captivated her. She aspires to be an astronaut.

In 2019, the world took notice. Forbes Mexico named her one of the 100 Most Powerful Women, recognizing her as a trailblazer. Top universities asked her to speak. She shared her story with large crowds. Her message was clear: Autism isn't a limitation. It's a unique way of seeing the universe and shaping it.

Adhara dreams of walking on the moon or exploring Mars. She studies hard and inspires others. She encourages them to accept themselves and aim high. Adhara Pérez's story goes beyond reaching for the stars. She reminds us that our brightest light comes from within.

TOM STOLTMAN

STRONGMAN

Tom Stoltman stood before the Atlas Stones, the crowd waiting in silence. The weight in front of him was massive, but that had never stopped him before. Every lift, every record, was proof of what discipline and belief could do. He stayed focused. His training guided each move. The stone inched higher, his long arms wrapping around it like it was made for him. With one final push, he placed it onto the platform. The stadium erupted in cheers. Another record. Another victory.

Tom was diagnosed with autism at age five. School was tough at times, as traditional classrooms were frustrating. He found comfort in sports. The routines were clear, and he could measure his progress. Football was his first love. As time passed, a different sport grabbed his attention.

At 16, he saw his older brother, Luke Stoltman, compete in strongman events. Watching his brother lift heavy weights and push his limits inspired him. Tom stepped into the gym, lifting for the first time. The weights didn't judge. They followed rules. They responded to discipline and effort. He felt at home. He trained hard with Luke's guidance.

At 18, Tom entered Scotland's Strongest Man. This marked the start of an amazing journey. His rise was swift. He dominated the Atlas Stones, turning them into his signature event. In 2021, he became the first Scot to win World's Strongest Man. The next year, he defended his title, proving it wasn't luck. In 2024, he won again, securing his legacy among the greatest strongmen in history.

Tom's success isn't only about records and trophies. He discusses his autism openly, referring to it as his "superpower." His story shows that true greatness isn't about being the strongest. It's about standing tall and knowing yourself. Push forward, no matter the weight ahead.

HIKARI ŌE

COMPOSER

Hikari Oe sat at the piano, his fingers gliding over the keys. The room was silent, except for the music that filled it with emotion and meaning. Music was his way of speaking, feeling, and thriving. Every note he played told a story, weaving beauty and hope into the air. The melodies reflected his thoughts, struggles, and dreams. For Hikari, the piano was a bridge to the world. His music let him express what words could not. It created a strong connection that touched the hearts of listeners.

Born in Japan in 1963, Hikari faced challenges from the start. He was born with a brain injury that caused developmental delays and was later diagnosed with autism. Doctors told his parents that he might never speak or live on his own. His parents, Kenzaburō Ōe, a famous novelist, and Yukari Ōe, would not let that define him. They supported him with love and provided opportunities to grow. This sparked his creativity.

As a child, Hikari showed little interest in most activities. Then, one day, he discovered the piano. The simple act of playing sparked something in him. Bird songs fascinated him. He played their melodies on the keys. This small curiosity grew into a love for composing. Hikari found it hard to communicate, but his love for music became his strength. It allowed him to express thoughts and emotions he couldn't put into words.

Hikari's music grew richer as he matured. By his early twenties, orchestras were already playing his music. People esteemed his pieces in Japan and across the globe. Critics praised his music for its depth and emotional power. For his parents, it was a triumph to see their son shine in ways they had never imagined.

Hikari Oe's music connects his inner world to listeners everywhere. His melodies reveal that true greatness stems from hard work and being true to oneself.

NEW ORLEANS
21

TONY SNELL

PROFESSIONAL BASKETBALL PLAYER

Tony Snell stood at the free-throw line, the basketball resting in his hands. The arena buzzed with anticipation, but Tony's focus was unshakable. He took a deep breath, ignored the noise, and released the ball. The swish of the net was a sound he knew well. It showed his dedication and calm under pressure. At 31, Tony learned something new about himself: he was on the autism spectrum.

Tony grew up in a tough neighborhood in Los Angeles. He always felt a bit different. Basketball was his refuge. It let him share his feelings without speaking. His hard work helped him shine at Martin Luther King High School in Riverside. There, he played with future NBA star Kawhi Leonard. After high school, Tony played at the University of New Mexico. His performance impressed NBA scouts. In 2013, the Chicago Bulls picked him with the 20th pick in the NBA Draft. His talent on the court was undeniable, leading him to a successful career in the NBA. His shooting and defense made him a key player on every team.

Later, Tony saw similarities in his life after doctors diagnosed his son, Karter, with autism. This made him want to get evaluated. He found out he was autistic, too. The diagnosis brought clarity to many of Tony's life experiences. Knowing about his own neurodiversity helped him connect better with his son and others like him. Tony embraced this new part of himself. He became an advocate for autism awareness. He started the Tony Snell Foundation to help children with autism and their families. The foundation provides resources and promotes understanding.

Tony Snell's journey highlights the power of self-discovery and acceptance. He shares his story to challenge misconceptions about autism. He shows that neurodiversity isn't a barrier; it's a different way to experience the world.

SUSAN BOYLE

SINGER

Susan Boyle stood on the stage of *Britain's Got Talent*, facing a skeptical audience and a panel of judges. The murmurs and doubtful glances didn't deter her. Taking a deep breath, she began to sing "I Dreamed a Dream" from *Les Misérables*. Her strong voice filled the theater. It changed doubt into wonder. When she finished, the crowd erupted in cheers. Susan's life changed.

Growing up in Scotland, Susan faced challenges that set her apart. Doctors misdiagnosed her with a learning disability from birth, so she often felt lost. Music became her refuge, a way to express herself when words fell short. With her mother's support, Susan improved her singing. She sang at local venues and church events. She loved what she did, but chances were few. So, she lived quietly, taking care of her elderly mother.

In 2009, at the age of 47, Susan took a courageous step by auditioning for *Britain's Got Talent*. Her performance amazed the judges and reached a global audience, gaining millions of views online. In one night, she became a sensation. Her debut album, "I Dreamed a Dream," topped charts around the world. It even became the fastest-selling debut album in UK history. In 2012, Susan learned she had Asperger's syndrome, a type of autism. She sought clarity about her lifelong struggles. This diagnosis brought relief and clarity. It helped her manage her condition better.

Susan faced personal and professional challenges, but her love for music stayed strong. She released more albums, performed for top audiences, and even tried acting. Her genuine nature and strength won her fans all over the world.

Susan Boyle's story shows the power of resilience and authenticity. It reminds us that it's never too late to chase our dreams. Her journey inspires millions. It proves that with talent and determination, amazing changes can happen.

USA
BRANNIGAN
3

MIKEY BRANNIGAN

PARALYMPIC RUNNER

The final turn was fast approaching. Mikey Brannigan surged forward, his legs on fire, his breathing sharp. Every mile, every sprint, every moment of exhaustion had led him to this instant. The crowd's roar was distant. His world was the rhythm of his strides, the pounding of his feet against the track. The finish line loomed ahead, and nothing could stop him now.

Born in East Northport, New York, in 1996, Mikey was diagnosed with autism at 18 months. Words came slowly, and communication was a struggle. At eight years old, he discovered the track, finding a new way to express himself. Running became his language, his way to show the world what he was capable of.

In high school, Mikey's talent became undeniable. He won two national championships. He led Northport High School to victory in major track events. His speed exceeded all expectations. It showed that athletic ability has no limits. However, the traditional classroom setting wasn't the right fit for him. Instead of giving up, Mikey turned professional in 2015, choosing to chase his dream on his own terms.

Mikey made history at age 19. He was the first T20-classified athlete to run a mile in under four minutes. His time was an impressive 3:57.58. Then, in 2016, he took the world stage at the Rio Paralympics. Mikey was in a tough race, but he kept his lead. He crossed the finish line first in the 1,500 meters, winning a gold medal for Team USA. His relentless drive made him a role model for athletes everywhere.

Mikey Brannigan shows that labels don't define what you can achieve. His story isn't about winning races; it's about proving that no finish line is out of reach. His speed, focus, and determination show the world that when passion meets perseverance, limits disappear.

INCLUSION
AND
AUTISM

MORÉNIKE GIWA ONAIWU

ADVOCATE

Morénike faced a packed audience at the United Nations. The weight of her journey filled her voice. She shared her experiences as a disabled person of color. She advocates for those whose voices are often unheard. Her journey to this moment has had many challenges. Yet, her strong commitment to justice and inclusion has led her here.

She was born in the United States to parents from Nigeria and Cape Verde. From a young age, she dealt with misunderstandings. People often misunderstood her unique behaviors. They believed these were cultural differences. They didn't see they were signs of autism. She didn't get her autism diagnosis until adulthood. This happened after her own children were diagnosed. This revelation brought clarity. It also showed the biases that had hidden her reality for a long time.

Determined to make a difference, she used her experiences to advocate for change. She founded Advocacy Without Borders. This nonprofit is all about inclusion and human rights. She helps people from various backgrounds. She ensures that everyone's voice counts in activism.

Morénike is a great writer and scholar. She has co-edited important works like *"Sincerely, Your Autistic Child"* and *"All the Weight of Our Dreams."* These collections show the experiences of autistic people, especially those of color. Her writings shine a light on many. They help close gaps in understanding and promote empathy.

Morénike's work has taken her to many important places. She has spoken at the White House and at events around the world. She proves that accepting who you are can turn challenges into strengths. She is working hard to make the world fairer and more welcoming for all.

自閉症者にも
心がある。
理解されるこ
とが大切です

NAOKI HIGASHIDO

AUTHOR

Naoki Higashida sat at his desk. His fingers hovered above a handmade alphabet grid. The room was quiet, but his mind buzzed with thoughts that he wanted to share. At 13, Naoki found a way to communicate through this grid, opening a door to the world. Writing became his voice. Through it, he shared feelings and ideas that had once been trapped inside him.

Born in Kimitsu, Japan, in 1992, Naoki was diagnosed with severe autism at five years old. He found traditional speech hard. One day, he discovered an alphabet grid. He pointed to letters to build sentences and share his thoughts. His mother encouraged him to write. He started making poems and short stories. He poured his experiences into his art.

In 2007, Naoki wrote "*The Reason I Jump*." This book shows what it's like to think as a person with autism. He shares his behaviors, challenges, and views through questions and answers. The book won praise around the world. This became even more true after the book was translated into English in 2013. It has been published in more than 30 languages. Readers around the world connect with it.

Naoki has written many other books, including "*Fall Down 7 Times Get Up 8*," published in 2015. This collection of essays shares his thoughts on identity, family, and society. His work provides comfort to families and individuals impacted by autism. It also challenges how society views nonverbal people.

Naoki went from being a nonverbal child to an author whose words have touched the world. His story shows that communication has many forms. Every voice should be heard. With patience, the right tools, and support, people with autism can break barriers. His journey pushes society to listen, adapt, and embrace the many ways we express ourselves.

Fisher
NEW YORK

TONY DEBLOIS

MUSICIAN

Tony DeBlois sat at the piano, fingers hovering lightly over the keys. He couldn't see the instrument. As he pressed down gently, music filled the room like sunlight pouring through a window. Each note he played was clear, strong, and effortless. Tony didn't need to see the piano keys. He knew exactly where each note lived. His fingers knew exactly what to do.

Tony was born weighing less than two pounds. He faced many challenges early on. Too much oxygen, which he needed to live, caused his blindness. As he grew, it was clear that traditional communication was hard for him. A toy organ bought at a yard sale showcased his amazing musical talent. At two years old, he played "Twinkle, Twinkle, Little Star" with ease. By the time he was five, Tony could play entire pieces after hearing them once. He soaked up music like a sponge, remembering thousands of songs in many genres. Janice saw her son's talent and nurtured it. She added music to his daily learning and growth.

Tony loves music and has mastered more than 20 instruments. He especially enjoys playing jazz piano. He has mastered more than 8,000 songs. They range from Beethoven to The Beatles. He faced disabilities but still sought education. He went to the Perkins School for the Blind. Later, he earned a magna cum laude degree from Berklee College of Music in 1996.

Tony has performed around the world. He shares his music. His talent and resilience inspire audiences. His life story appeared in the 1997 CBS movie "Journey of the Heart." It showed the challenges and triumphs he and his mother faced.

Tony DeBlois's journey is a testament to dedication and belief. His music crosses barriers. It touches hearts everywhere. With passion and hard work, he turns obstacles into lasting melodies.

DR. MARY DOHERTY

PHYSICIAN

Dr. Mary Doherty walked quickly through the busy hospital hallway, holding her medical notes tightly. Nurses and doctors hurried past her, each rushing to their tasks. Suddenly, an urgent call came over the speaker. A patient needed help right away in the operating room. Mary felt her heart beating faster, but she didn't panic. She stayed calm and clear-headed. She knew exactly what to do next. Everyone trusted Mary during emergencies because she always stayed strong and focused. Her ability to handle stress came from her experience of living with autism.

Born in Ireland, Mary always felt comfortable in places with clear rules and routines. That's why she decided to become an anesthesiologist, a doctor who helps patients sleep safely during surgery. Mary was diagnosed with autism in her mid-forties. This explained many things about her life. Autism shaped the way she paid attention to details, helping her become a great doctor.

Mary wanted to connect with other doctors who were autistic like her. In 2019, she started a group called Autistic Doctors International (ADI). This global network offers peer support and advocates for neurodiversity in medicine. Creating a space for autistic doctors to share their stories and experiences. ADI also teaches people about autism.

Mary does even more. She helps autistic patients get better medical care. Her research shows that patients with autism often face extra challenges at the doctor. She helps doctors understand how people with autism feel and what they need.

By accepting who she is, Mary has made medicine better for everyone. Her work teaches us something important: when we listen to and understand each other, amazing things can happen.

KC
Royals
22

TARIK EL-ABOUR

BASEBALL PLAYER

Tarik El-Abour adjusted his stance, gripping the bat tighter. The pitcher wound up, the seams of the baseball spinning fast toward home plate. Tarik wasn't thinking about the crowd, the expectations, or the path that led him here. His focus was on the ball—tracking it, timing it, making contact. In baseball, skills matter more than words. He swung. The crack of the bat sent the ball soaring, but it was more than just a hit. It was proof that he belonged. Proof that the game welcomed players like him. And proof that he had broken the limits set on him long ago.

Diagnosed with autism at three, Tarik faced challenges that should have stopped him in his tracks. He didn't speak until he was six. A chance encounter with a baseball game on television ignited a spark in him. At ten, he picked up a bat for the first time. He faced some struggles, but he stayed dedicated. With his mother, Nadia, always by his side, Tarik was taught to concentrate on his strengths. She believed in his abilities. So, he practiced hard.

After high school, he encountered setbacks, such as being cut from college teams. He didn't give up. Instead, he transferred to Bristol University to play baseball, where he also earned a Business Administration degree. His persistence took him to the independent Empire League, where he excelled. He earned Rookie of the Year honors with a .323 batting average for the Sullivan Explorers. His performance caught the Kansas City Royals' attention. In 2018, he signed a Minor League contract, making him one of the first known professional baseball players with autism.

Tarik El-Abour's story shows how passion, resilience, and support can turn challenges into successes. His achievements challenge how society views autism. They prove that, with help and determination, people can break barriers. Tarik's journey inspires many to chase their dreams despite the odds.

Ranveer Saini
India

RANVEER SINGH SAINI

GOLFER

Ranveer Singh Saini stood on the green, holding his club firmly. The world around him faded—the chatter, the movement, the noise. All that mattered was the ball, the target, and the swing. He took a deep breath, adjusting his stance. Years of training had led to this moment. As the club met the ball with a crisp, perfect strike, the crowd erupted. This wasn't luck. This was precision, practice, and a mind built for the game.

At age two, Ranveer was diagnosed with autism. His parents looked for ways to help him focus, and that's when he found golf. The sport's structure, patience, and rhythm fit him in a way nothing else had. Every putt, every drive, and every round sharpened his focus. What started as practice soon turned into something more—he was good. Very good.

That talent carried him on to the world stage. He made history in 2015 when he won India's first gold medal in golf at the Special Olympics World Games in Los Angeles. His victory shattered expectations and inspired athletes across the country. But he wasn't finished. He kept competing in the following years. He won a silver medal at the 2019 World Games in Abu Dhabi. Then, he earned a gold medal at the 2023 World Games in Berlin. He earned the Bhim Award in 2017 and the Shreshth Divyangjan Award in 2024. These are two of India's top honors for athletes with disabilities.

Beyond the medals, Ranveer's story is about more than golf. It's about breaking barriers. Talent and determination matter more than labels. His success has inspired more children with autism to try sports. It shows them that, with the right help, they can shine too. His journey shows that focus, patience, and self-belief can make dreams come true.

JONATHAN LERMAN

ARTIST

Jonathan Lerman sat at his desk with charcoal in hand. He fixed his eyes on the blank paper. His fingers moved with speed, each stroke creating a face. Lines turned into deep eyes, textured skin, and lively faces. Without a word, Jonathan told stories through his art. His art showed the world how he felt inside.

Jonathan, born in 1987, received an autism diagnosis at two years old. As a child, he didn't speak much, and the world around him often seemed overwhelming. Talking was hard for him, but he connected with art right away. He grabbed a pencil and started drawing portraits. His work had amazing detail and depth, even without training. By the time he was 10, Jonathan's sketches stunned those around him. His work had a unique style. It was raw, expressive, and very emotional. His skill in capturing faces with such vivid detail made people stop and stare. His art showed the thoughts and feelings of his subjects.

His talent didn't go unnoticed. At 14, galleries all over the U.S. showcased Jonathan's art. Critics loved how he captured emotions on paper. They compared him to well-known artists who had unique views. His drawings were haunting yet vibrant. They urged people to see the world as he did.Jonathan's success grew as more people noticed his art. His work appeared in big exhibitions. Collectors looked for his pieces. His story became a source of inspiration. He demonstrated that creativity has no bounds.

Jonathan Lerman's sketches show truths that words can't say. Each stroke of his charcoal captures something deeper—an unspoken emotion, a hidden story, a glimpse into the soul. His portraits show more than faces. They capture the weight of experience, the depth of feeling, and the quiet humanity in each subject. They show us that the most powerful stories aren't always told with words.

DR. TEMPLE GRANDIN

ANIMAL SCIENTIST

Dr. Temple Grandin stood at the edge of the cattle pen, her eyes tracking the movement of the herd. She saw patterns in how the animals acted. They responded to their surroundings, moved instinctively, and sent silent signals. She had a deep understanding of their language. She noticed details that others often missed. What many saw as a challenge became her greatest strength. She changed the livestock industry by creating humane systems. These designs helped reduce stress for animals everywhere.

Temple's childhood came with challenges. Diagnosed with autism as a child, she didn't start talking until she was almost four. Everything changed when she visited her aunt's ranch in Arizona. She found clarity there. She found it fascinating to watch how cattle moved. Their subtle behavior changes and reactions to their surroundings intrigued her. She saw that by knowing their needs, she could create better, kinder systems to help keep them calm. This discovery changed her life and the livestock industry for good.

Dr. Grandin created curved chute systems and other tools to lessen stress for animals during handling. She helped ranchers build facilities that focused on animal well-being. Her designs are now used around the world. She showed that caring for animals is ethical and helps farmers get better results.

Temple Grandin's life shows that thinking differently can change the world. Her work has helped millions of animals and inspired many people. She reminds us that each mind has a distinct perspective on the world. Sometimes, these differences spark the greatest breakthroughs.

BRITISH

JESSICA-JANE APPLEGATE

PARALYMPIC SWIMMER

Jessica-Jane Applegate stood at the pool's edge. The water sparkled under the arena's bright lights. The sound of cheers echoed through the air as she adjusted her goggles and took a deep breath. The whistle blew. Jessica dove in and swam with strong, steady strokes. For her, the pool was a place of clarity and focus. A space where she could thrive.

Jessica was born in Great Yarmouth, England. She always felt connected to water. As a child, she loved swimming, finding peace and freedom in the water. Jessica was diagnosed with autism as a teen. She struggled to keep up with the fast-paced world. The rhythm of her strokes and the silence beneath the surface bring her a sense of calm.

Her natural talent and drive made her stand out. Coaches saw her strong work ethic and focus while under pressure. By young adulthood, she was competing at top levels in para-swimming events. She didn't just swim, she smashed records. At 16, she competed for Great Britain in the 2012 London Paralympics. She won gold in the 200-meter freestyle. This win was a personal triumph and a historic moment. She became the first autistic athlete to win Paralympic gold for Great Britain.

There was even greater success in the years that followed. Jessica won many medals at international competitions. Her dedication and resilience inspired countless people. She also became a role model for young athletes, especially those with autism. She proved that being different is a strength. With hard work and belief, anything is possible.

Jessica-Jane Applegate's journey reminds us of the power of perseverance. She inspires others to chase their dreams, despite the challenges they face. Through every stroke, she proves that greatness comes from embracing who you are.

JORY FLEMING

CLIMATE SCIENTIST

Jory Fleming sat at his desk, staring at the map on his computer screen. Each road, river, and coastline held a special significance. They fit together like pieces of a puzzle. Patterns and connections emerge through geography. Stories that lie beneath the surface are uncovered. Jory has a remarkable talent for spotting details. He notices connections that others may miss. To him, the world's complexity becomes clearer through maps.

Born in South Carolina in 1995, Jory was diagnosed with autism at the age of five. He has a unique perspective on the world. He sees details that often go unnoticed. Routines and structure make him feel secure. Unpredictable moments can be tough. In his book, *How to Be Human: An Autistic Man's Guide to Life*, Jory shares how certain situations can be draining for him. Social interactions and daily tasks sometimes feel exhausting. However, maps bring him clarity in our fast-paced world. Geography helps him understand his surroundings.

Despite facing challenges, Jory thrived in school. He discovered strength in his ability to concentrate. His mother played a key role in nurturing his curiosity, helping him create plans that suited his learning style. Alongside her support, Jory also found comfort in his service dog, Daisy. She helped him navigate daily life. She offered companionship and a sense of safety in tough times.

In 2017, Jory achieved a remarkable milestone. He became the first autistic student from South Carolina to win the Rhodes Scholarship. He studied geographic information systems at the University of Oxford. This field uses maps and data to tackle big problems, like climate change and conservation. He transformed his unique way of thinking into a powerful tool for making a difference.

CHRIS PACKHAM

WILDLIFE EXPERT

Chris Packham crouched in the tall grass, holding his breath. A few feet away, a fox stood still, ears twitching, eyes fixed on him. Most would have moved and startled the fox, but Chris stayed motionless. He had learned to stay still and observe. This skill helped him perceive the world in a unique way. As a naturalist, Chris spent many hours studying wildlife. He observed everything from majestic birds of prey to clever urban foxes. This experience taught him to slow down, wait, and watch. He discovered that stillness and silence could reveal hidden secrets. The natural world was full of surprises waiting to be discovered.

Growing up in England, Chris found his true home in nature. He wandered through forests. He collected fossils and studied birds for hours. The natural world felt clear to him. Crowded places and loud noises overwhelmed him. He found solace in the quiet beauty of the outdoors. For years, Chris felt different but didn't know why. He was diagnosed with autism only after he reached adulthood. That was when the puzzle pieces of his childhood clicked into place.

Chris turned his passion into a great career. He became a wildlife expert, photographer, and TV presenter. As the host of Springwatch, he shared nature's wonders with millions. He inspired viewers to appreciate and protect the environment. Through his vibrant stories and enthusiasm, Chris brought people closer to nature.

Chris became a strong advocate for autism awareness. He used his stage to share his experiences and challenge common misconceptions. He proved that being different is a strength, not a weakness. By sharing his journey, he gave hope to many people and families facing similar struggles. Often, the greatest discoveries come from viewing the world through your own lens.

STEPHEN WILTSHIRE

ARTIST

Stephen Wiltshire stood in front of a large canvas, the fresh scent of paper around him. He closed his eyes and pictured the city's skyline from the helicopter ride a few hours ago. He remembered every window, roof, and street. After a deep breath, he opened his eyes and started to draw. Lines flowed with grace, buildings emerged steadily, and a detailed cityscape gradually took form. For Stephen, this was more than art. It was his voice and a connection to a world he once felt was far away and unwelcoming.

As a child, Stephen faced significant challenges. Diagnosed with autism at the age of three, he was nonverbal and found it difficult to relate to others. His world was silent but rich with images and patterns. At five, he started at Queensmill School in London. There, teachers saw his amazing drawing talent. They encouraged him, using art as a bridge to communication. Remarkably, his first word was "paper," a testament to his profound connection to his craft.

Stephen can recall and recreate complex cityscapes from memory. He can observe a city once and then draw it in meticulous detail. This extraordinary skill has led him to create panoramic drawings of some of the world's most iconic cities, including Tokyo, Rome, Hong Kong, and New York. His 19-foot-long picture of New York City shows his amazing talent.

In 2006, Stephen received the Member of the Order of the British Empire (MBE) for his art contributions. That year, he also opened a permanent gallery in London's Royal Opera Arcade. Visitors from all over the world admire his detailed cityscapes there. Stephen's journey shows us the importance of nurturing individual talents. Sometimes, the most profound stories are told without words.

"Hope" is the thing with feathers -
That perches in the soul -
And sings the tune without the words -
And never stops - at all -

And sweetest - in the Gale - is heard -
And sore must be the storm -
That could abash the little Bird
That kept so many warm -

I've heard it in the chillest land -
And on the strangest Sea -
Yet - never - in Extremity,
It asked a crumb - of me.

EMILY DICKENSON
POET

Emily Dickinson sat by her window, sunlight shining onto her desk. She held a piece of paper in her hands and wrote meaningful words with great attention. Her home in Amherst, Massachusetts, was calm and serene. Emily loved the stillness. It gave her time to think, imagine, and create. Her poems helped her make sense of life. They were a way to share her thoughts with everyone.

Emily was born in 1830. She didn't live like most people her age. Emily stayed home while others went to gatherings. She enjoyed being alone, reading, and writing. The world outside often felt too busy, but she found comfort in her own thoughts. Some researchers believe Emily may have been autistic. Her strong focus, love of routine, and preference for being alone support this idea. Yet, there is no way to confirm it.

Emily's poetry was unlike anything people had seen before. She didn't follow the usual rules of writing. She used dashes, not commas. She wrote in short lines. She shared her feelings courageously and sincerely. Her poems talked about nature, love, and even death. Emily saw beauty in small moments, like the way a bird moves or how the seasons change.

Emily wrote hundreds of poems, but she published only a few during her life. She didn't write to become famous. Writing was something she did for herself. After she passed away in 1886, her family found hundreds of her poems tucked away. Her sister, Lavinia, helped share them with the world.

Many view Emily Dickinson as one of America's greatest poets. Her work continues to inspire people all over the world. Emily's story reminds us that being different is a gift. Sometimes, the most powerful voices are the quiet ones. Her poems show us how to see beauty in everyday life and how to express our thoughts in our own unique way.

DANI BOWMAN

ANIMATOR

Dani Bowman sat at her desk, pencil in hand, bringing characters to life. With each line she sketched, a new story unfolded, vibrant and full of energy. For Dani, animation was more than art. It was her passion and purpose. It was her way to brighten the world.

Dani discovered animation at 11 years old and was immediately hooked. While other kids were watching cartoons, Dani was learning how to make them. She spent countless hours drawing, storyboarding, and crafting short films. Her sharp focus and endless creativity gave her an edge. This helped her bring her imaginative worlds to life. She wasn't creating for herself. She wanted her art to connect with people and bring them joy.

At 14, Dani started her animation company, DaniMation Entertainment. She ran workshops, made films, and built her career. She taught animation to young people with autism. She showed them that their focus and creativity was a strength. Her workshops taught skills and built confidence and community. Dani's knack for uplifting others was crucial to her journey and her success in art.

Over 40 international film festivals have shown Dani's animated shorts. She has worked with major organizations to promote inclusion through creativity. Dani partners with companies and nonprofits to showcase the talents of autistic individuals. Her work has affected lives worldwide. Dani believes that autism isn't a limitation, it's a unique perspective on life.

Dani continues to grow her company. She mentors future animators and advocates for autistic individuals in creative fields. Her work reminds us that the most inspiring stories often come from those who dare to think outside the box.

619

DAVID CAMPION

SNOWBOARDER

David Campion stood at the top of the slope, the crisp mountain air filling his lungs. The snow sparkled under the sunlight, a blank canvas waiting for his next run. As he tightened the straps on his snowboard, his mind honed in on the path ahead. Snowboarding was more than a sport for David. It was his way of experiencing a deep sense of being alive.

Born in Australia, David discovered snowboarding at a young age. Diagnosed with autism as a child, he found solace in the structure and rhythm of the sport. Snowboarding gave him clarity in an unpredictable world. Each turn, jump, and carve let him connect with the mountain. It was a way to express himself beyond words.

David's talent on the slopes was clear. His focus and precision helped him read terrain and adapt to snow changes. As he practiced more, the snowboarding community took notice. His technical skill and natural feel for the mountain made him stand out from other athletes.

In 2017, David represented Australia at the Special Olympics World Winter Games in Austria. He showcased his skills on an international stage. Competing with top snowboarders, he delivered standout performances. These earned him recognition and respect. For David, each run was a chance to push his limits and show his true potential.

David's journey as a snowboarder is a testament to his dedication and passion for the sport. His story shows that greatness comes from using your strengths. It's about pursuing what brings you real freedom. For David, the slopes are not a challenge, they are home.

We're Not Broke

ERIC GARCIA

JOURNALIST

Eric Garcia sat at his desk, the soft glow of his computer screen illuminating his face. Stacks of notes and books surrounded him. As a political journalist in Washington, D.C., his thoughts whirled like a storm. The newsroom buzzed with urgency. Deadlines loomed, but Eric thrived amid the chaos. He built a career studying how policy, economics, politics, and people connect. Eric's true goal went beyond the headlines. He wanted to change how the world sees autism. To him, journalism was more than a job, it was a way to make a difference.

Eric was diagnosed with autism when he was a child. He faced many misconceptions from society. He often heard people say that they should cure autism as if it were an illness. This view never matched his experiences. Instead of seeing autism as a limitation, he viewed it as a key part of who he is.

In 2021, Eric wrote a book called *We're Not Broken: Changing the Autism Conversation*. He used interviews and personal reflections to show the diverse experiences of autistic individuals in America. His work challenged common myths. He emphasized that autistic people don't need fixing, they need understanding and support.

Eric also became a key voice in journalism. He wrote for major publications and joined talks about autism and policy. His reporting made neurodiversity a national topic. He shared a viewpoint that was often overlooked. He made room for autistic voices to be acknowledged and valued.

Eric Garcia keeps sharing his message. He inspires others. He shows that being true to yourself can spark real change. He's building a future where people listen to and value autistic voices. True progress happens when everyone gets a chance to succeed.

2012 BIG TEN TOURNAMENT
CHAMPIONS
SPARTANS.
44
BIG TEN

ANTHONY IANNI

COLLEGE ATHLETE & ADVOCATE

Anthony Ianni stood on the basketball court, the crowd's roar echoing around him. He gripped the ball, took a deep breath, and focused his mind. His whole life, people had doubted him, but he had spent years proving them wrong.

As a child, Anthony faced challenges that few understood. Diagnosed with autism at age four, doctors told his parents that his future would have limits. They warned he might never graduate from high school, live on his own, or hold a career.

Basketball became his passion. The game gave him focus, discipline, and purpose. On the court, he found a place where the doubts of others didn't matter. The road was tough. Coaches questioned if he could handle the game's intensity. Opponents underestimated him, focusing only on his challenges. Instead of feeling discouraged, Anthony worked harder. He spent hours practicing his shots, boosting his stamina, and building strength. He stayed late after practice. The ball echoed in the empty gym while he perfected his shots. Every doubt fueled his drive to succeed.

His hard work paid off in surprising ways. He became the first known autistic athlete to play Division I college basketball. At Michigan State University, he played for the legendary coach Tom Izzo and alongside future Golden State Warrior, Draymond Green.

Anthony's impact continued after his basketball career. He dedicated his life to helping others, taking a stand against the bullying of autistic kids and speaking up for those who felt unheard. His goal was to inspire students, athletes, and families. His message was clear: Never let anyone limit what you can achieve. His story shows us that with enough determination, we can achieve greatness no matter what obstacles we face.

CLAY MARZO

SURFER

Clay Marzo stood on his surfboard. His eyes were fixed on the rolling waves. The ocean roared around him, but Clay felt completely calm. He moved smoothly across the water, turning with ease and confidence. Each wave carried him closer to peace. When Clay surfed, he shared his true self with the world.

Growing up in Maui, Clay loved being near the ocean. It made him feel relaxed and happy. Clay received an autism diagnosis at the age of 18. This helped him make sense of the challenges he had faced his whole life. For Clay, the diagnosis wasn't a restriction, it was an answer. It gave him the clarity to accept himself and focus even more on the one thing that brought him freedom- the ocean.

Clay had a natural gift for surfing. He redefined the sport. His smooth, natural style made him one of the most creative surfers of his time. At 15, he won the NSSA National Championship. He achieved a perfect score, which put him in the spotlight. Shortly after, he turned professional, competing against the best surfers in the world. He was known for riding barrels with great precision. His maneuvers amazed even the most seasoned surfers. Clay appeared in major surf films like *Just Add Water*. This film showcased his talent and unique style in the sport. He won many championships. People know him as one of the most innovative surfers of his time.

Clay's journey included more than championships and awards. He became an advocate for autism awareness. He inspires young people with autism to find their passions and embrace them. His own journey shows that the ocean, much like life, rewards those who go with the flow and stay true to themselves. Clay continues to ride waves and inspires others. He shows us that true greatness comes from facing life with courage and confidence.

GOODYEAR
NASCAR
GOODYEAR
SUNOCO
ARCA
UNOH
28
RACE 4 AUTISM
Sioux Chief
SUNOCO
UNOH
MENARDS
GOODYEAR

ARMANI WILLIAMS

NASCAR DRIVER

Armani Williams gripped the steering wheel tightly. The powerful engine roared to life around him. He took a deep breath, feeling the vibration of the car beneath him. The racetrack stretched ahead, filled with noise and excitement, but Armani felt calm. Racing was how Armani showed the world that he belonged there.

At just two years old, Armani was diagnosed with autism. Doctors warned his parents that lifelong communication and social challenges could define his future. Yet, Armani had a passion that stood out—he loved cars. He could watch races for hours, studying every detail of the drivers and their machines. This fascination was more than a hobby, it was a spark of something greater.

As he got older, that spark turned into determination. Armani wanted to drive. Learning to drive was tough. The sounds and vibrations can overwhelm even the most experienced pros. For someone with heightened sensory sensitivity, the challenge was bigger. He spent years perfecting his skills. He gained confidence and mastered the focus needed for racing.

His relentless effort paid off. Armani became the first known autistic professional race car driver, competing in NASCAR. On the track, he didn't just compete, he excelled. His speed and precision impressed fans and other drivers. His ability to remain calm under pressure and push through challenges earned him respect in the racing world.

Armani's impact goes beyond the racetrack. He started sharing his story with young people, especially those with autism. He encourages them to follow their passions, no matter what the odds. Through his platform, he has helped many groups that promote autism awareness and inclusion. He uses his voice and success to create change.

Miss America 2012
MISS MONTANA

ALEXIS WINEMAN

BEAUTY QUEEN

Alexis Wineman stood backstage, her heart racing. Bright lights shined through the curtains. She could hear the excited crowd talking and clapping. Alexis took a deep breath and stood tall. She was about to step on stage and speak for people who were rarely heard.

Alexis had always seen the world from a unique perspective. Her mind worked in a different way, focusing on details that others missed. She was diagnosed with autism at 11. She found that focusing on what mattered was one of her biggest strengths. This trait fueled her journey. She chased her goals with clear focus and strong determination.

When she discovered public speaking, everything fell into place. The words that once seemed elusive became her most powerful tool. Alexis shared her views to inspire understanding, especially about autism. She sparked important conversations that people had overlooked.

At 18, she joined the Miss America pageant. She was the first contestant with autism to compete. This was a big deal. The Miss America stage had bright lights and loud crowds. It was an intense place. Alexis faced it with poise and courage. Her confidence and authenticity won hearts across the nation.

Winning Miss Montana in 2012 was not only a personal win. It marked a moment of representation and empowerment. Alexis didn't go to the Miss America stage to conform. She aimed to change how people view beauty, potential, and autism. Her presence was not only groundbreaking but also transformative.

Alexis continues to inspire many. She shares her story and stands up for the inclusion and acceptance of people with autism. She shows us that true beauty lies in authenticity, and that every voice has the power to make a difference.

TELL THE WORLD YOUR STORY

Everyone in this book has a story that makes them shine. Now it's your turn. Use this page to tell the world about your story.

Every part of you matters. Write about what makes you, *you*.

PICTURE YOUR GREATNESS

Use this space to draw something that represents your greatness. It could be a goal or how you see yourself changing the world.

Draw it. Snap a pic. Then share it and tag us! #TalesOfGreatness

📸 TikTok: **@tales_of_greatness_** 📸 Instagram: **@talesofgreatness**

ACKNOWLEDGEMENTS

To the extraordinary individuals featured in this book—thank you. Your willingness to share your stories with the world is an act of bravery. By making your journeys public, you are opening doors, breaking down barriers, and giving hope to so many others who deserve to see what's possible. Your achievements, your challenges, and your triumphs are a reminder that greatness comes in many forms, and the world is better because of you.

A special thank you to our illustrator, Iryna Kasianova. Whose talent and dedication brought these stories to life. From her home in Ukraine, Iryna balanced her work with autistic children by day and poured her heart into these illustrations by night. Her passion for this project runs deep, and every page reflects her care and creativity.

To those who want to dive deeper, you can learn more about the individuals in this book by visiting our **Beyond the Spectrum Blog** at *talesofgreatness.com*. Each person's journey doesn't end on these pages—there is always more to discover.

Thank you to everyone who believes in representation, inclusion, and diverse thinking. Your support makes this journey possible.

ABOUT THE AUTHOR

Syed Raza believes in the power of stories to change the way we see the world. As the creator of the Tales of Greatness publishing brand, Syed shares the journeys of extraordinary people who break barriers, challenge expectations, and show us what's possible when we embrace who we are.

With a deep commitment to inclusion and representation, Syed created this book to celebrate the brilliance, strength, and unique voices of the autistic community. He wants to inspire readers of all ages. He encourages them to dream big, break limits, and see the greatness inside themselves.

Beyond the page, Syed is building spaces—both online and in real life—where every person feels seen, every story is valued, and the next generation is encouraged to believe in their own power to make a difference.

Want more inspiring stories? Scan the QR code below to visit **talesofgreatness.com** and discover more books in the series!

Made in the USA
Columbia, SC
08 April 2025

56173637R00038